Hello fellow dog lover! I am Mina Saint, and I'm thrilled to introduce you to a world full of our furry friends in all their diverse glory. This book celebrates the incredible variety in the canine world - some you may be familiar with and others that will be delightful new discoveries.

In this coloring book, you will meet 50 different breeds of dogs, each with its charm and distinctive characteristics. Whether you're a fan of the noble German Shepherd, the playful Labrador Retriever, or eager to explore the unknown, you're in for a treat.

Here are a few tips to get the most out of your coloring adventure:

- **Try Different Mediums:** Feel free to experiment with crayons, colored pencils, markers, or watercolor. Remember to place a sheet of paper under the page you're coloring using markers or watercolor to prevent bleed-through.
- **No Rules Apply:** Remember, this is your creative journey! Don't be afraid to use unrealistic colors. Who says a dog can't be purple?
- **Take Your Time:** Savor the process. Each page is a chance to relax and express yourself. There's no rush to finish.
- **Test Your Tools:** Use the last page to test your colors before applying them to the pictures. This will help you visualize the final result better.

Most importantly, enjoy every moment of your coloring journey. Let the variety of dogs inspire you and spark your creativity.

If you enjoy your time with "Paws & Tails: Coloring Book," I would love to hear about your experience. Sharing your thoughts can help other coloring book enthusiasts find this book and help me create better coloring books in the future.

Thank you for embarking on this coloring adventure with me.

Happy coloring!

Mina Saint

Boerboel

Pug

Saint Bernard

Malteese

Chihuahua

Chow Chow

Poodle

Bulldog

Siberian Husky

French Bulldog

Komonder

Rottweiler

Border Collie

Pitbull

Lhaso Apso

Labradoodle

Beagle

Schnauzers

Chinese Crested

Great Dane

Sheepadoodle

Cardigan Welsh Corgi

Shih Tzu

Tibetan Mastiff

Mexican Hairless

Affenpinscher

Dachshund

Bergamasco Shepard

Boston Terriers

Irish Setter

Greyhound

Papillon

Belgian Malinois

Labrador Retriever

Bermese Mountain Dog

German Shepard

Yorkipoo

Boxer

Yorkshire Terrier

Dobermann

Pomeranians

Icelandic Sheepdog

Golden Retriever

Cavalier King Charles Spaniels

Cockapoo

Grand Basset Griffon Vendéen

Polish Lowland Sheepdog

Havanese

Cane Corso

American English Coonhound